THE OTHER
ISCARIOT

For my cousins Bonnie + Bill!

THE OTHER
ISCARIOT

FREDERICK CLINTON BURDICK

FCBurdick
Dec. 2014

TATE PUBLISHING
AND ENTERPRISES, LLC

Published by Tate Publishing & Enterprises, LLC
127 E. Trade Center Terrace | Mustang, Oklahoma 73064 USA
1.888.361.9473 | www.tatepublishing.com

Tate Publishing is committed to excellence in the publishing industry. The company reflects the philosophy established by the founders, based on Psalm 68:11,
"The Lord gave the word and great was the company of those who published it."

Book design copyright © 2014 by Tate Publishing, LLC. All rights reserved.
Cover design by Nikolai Purpura
Interior design by Joana Quilantang

Published in the United States of America

ISBN: 978-1-63185-555-9
1. Religion / Biblical Studies / Jesus, the Gospels & Acts
2. Religion / Biblical Commentary / New Testament
14.07.14

FOREWORD

In each of the four major gospels there are but three men listed by their full names: Judas Iscariot, the betrayer of Jesus to the High Priest; Pontius Pilate, who condemned Jesus to be crucified; and Simon Iscariot, father of Judas. Simon was of a generation earlier; what was his role relative to Jesus?

I believe that Judas Iscariot was taught by his father Simon that the Messiah had already been born; therefore, after his father's death Judas began his search for the "Holy One" in the land near the Jordan, where a great prophet named John was preaching and baptizing. On the day that Jesus and his eleven followers were clothing themselves after having been baptized, Judas asked John if he was the Messiah, and John pointed to Jesus, saying, "There is the holy one whose sandal I am not fit to loosen." Thereupon Judas asked Jesus if he could follow Him, and Jesus replied, "As you will," because He knew Judas to be his future betrayer and that Judas believed Him to be the long-promised Messiah.

The obvious question then is how did Judas' father Simon come to have such information, and thus begins my version of the nativity story about the birth of Jesus, and of Simon Iscariot, of the generation before in the court of King Herod.

PROLOGUE

The birth of the Son of God was not random, not accidental —it was a long-planned and well-executed event. The virgin mother-to-be was always "full of grace," even before God's beginning of human kind. The very planets had been started in orbits that would, millions of years after the Creation, bring them together in a confluence of light that shone one winter night above a small village in Judea. To move a humble carpenter and his expectant wife from one end of the promised land to the other would require the unwitting help of no less a person than the Emperor of the known world, who was moved to call for a counting of his subjects. And, to witness this birth of the Child, a threesome of mysterious stargazers and a few lowly shepherds will serve: the Prince of Heaven, Son of the Most High, was born in a manger and lived, seemingly unheralded, among his people! The account of the nativity of Jesus depends upon the gospel witnesses, Matthew and Luke. But from whom did Matthew get the nativity details?

From the only knowledgeable person still alive after the Crucifixion… Mary, full of grace, ever virgin mother of Christ and resolute keeper of many secrets in her heart! So, let us see…

THE CHRONOLOGY

Archangel Gabriel appears to the Blessed Virgin Mary to reveal God's plan for her to bear his only son. Caesar Augustus orders a census to be taken of all free men in the Roman Empire, to last a year in which every free man must register himself and his possessions at the place of his birth. The angel appears to Joseph to convince him that Mary will bear God's son by the Holy Spirit, that she has not committed adultery. Joseph thereafter accepts her into his home when she returns from her visit to her cousin Elisabeth, of whom the angel had spoken (in proof) of the birthing of her son John.

The angel comes separately to the Magi to invite each to observe the great star forming in the western skies, near Jerusalem. They are excited about the "great king" to be born.

Simon Iscariot gains favor with Herod, king of Jerusalem.

Joseph and Mary arrive in Bethlehem for him to register in the Roman census, where the Virgin Mary gives birth to her only son, Jesus. Having no rooms left, the innkeeper leads Joseph into the cave-like animal sanctuary carved out of the sandstone under the rear of the inn. The innkeeper's wife helps Mary, and offers to be her midwife during the long night ahead.

The Magi arrive in Jerusalem to question Herod's court as to the birthplace of the "new king." Herod's temple priests find an obscure prophet's (Isaiah) words that the "king" is to be born in Bethlehem, a city that a biblical king named David built. Herod, inwardly alarmed, asks the Magi to return to his court after finding the new "king," so that he too might worship the child to be born.

Angels appear during the night to announce the birth to shepherds, so they gather at the manger to see the child. Magi come to worship thereafter, bringing their gifts. Later, the angel warns the three Magi not to return to Herod in Jerusalem, but to return to their lands by another route.

After two days go by, Herod orders Iscariot, his chief of the palace guards, to go down to Bethlehem to look for the Magi. Iscariot reports back that he could find no one fitting their description. An angry Herod vows revenge for their disobedience, for he has been much frightened by the inquiries of these strange visitors about a "new King."

While Simon Iscariot travels to Bethlehem, on the eighth day after the Child's birth, Mary and Joseph journey in the opposite direction up to the temple in Jerusalem to present Jesus to the priests for circumcision, offering a pair of doves as their sacrifice.

In the Temple, Simeon and Anna celebrate the presentation of the Child, for them the long-promised Messiah!

And Mary keeps all these events in her heart. She and Joseph return on the road down to Bethlehem, intending to go north to Nazareth, from whence they had come.

Meanwhile, a vengeful Herod again sends Simon to Bethlehem with two of his least-desirable soldiers to kill all male children under two years of age, giving specific orders to Simon to kill the drunken soldiers after their bloody work. The mothers of the slain children, however, are not to be harmed!

Simon asks the innkeeper's wife to gather the mothers of new boys under age two, at the request of King Herod, to be sure that all Jewish sons are being properly circumcised. Having long been the local midwife, she is able to gather the six young mothers and their sons in the "great room" at the inn, two days later.

At the crossroads, after the presentation and circumcision of the Child, the angel warns Joseph that the Child and His mother are in great danger, so he is advised to take them down into Egypt to wait until it is safe to return. They begin the ascent up the south road. The road that turns down into Egypt is not far beyond.

The slaughter of the Innocents occurs, the fleeing soldiers are slain by Simon, who then overhears (from the very distraught innkeeper's wife) that a seventh male child has disappeared. Simon foresees his own fate if he returns, unsuccessful, to confront an angry Herod; he, too, must flee. He would set out for Egypt.

As Simon Iscariot mounts his horse to pursue the far-off figures of the carpenter, wife and child, the angel warns him, with great force, against coming near the Child and His mother.

THE PLAYERS

MARY AND JOSEPH, AND THE CHILD JESUS

Joseph was an itinerant carpenter, a large man, brawny from the kind of work that he did in both wood and stone, an honest, gentle and very quiet man who kept his peace, respected by others, devout in his attendance at synagogue, and charitable. His worth was great in the eyes of The Most High, for why else could he have been so chosen to be Mary's spouse, and assigned to her and the Child's protection by the Angel? Joseph had no doubts about the Angel's messages to him; he followed the Angel's instructions without question. He and his new wife would spend many hours talking about what their angel in common had said to each. They knew they were following the wishes of The Most High.

THE ARCHANGEL

Gabriel had been assigned by The Most High to make the whole nativity event occur, as foretold by the prophet (Isaiah) and afterward by the gospel writers (Matthew, Mark, and Luke). Their writings tell us that the Angel appeared once to Mary, three times to Joseph; certainly (and logically) the Angel came to others as well, e.g. Magi, shepherds, Emperor, etc.

THE INNKEEPER

He was a clever man in his middle years, taught by his father how to be a good host and a careful business man as well. He studied people closely, especially those who came into the courtyard of his inn to ask for lodging. To those he estimated would be able to pay for his room, he would give cheery welcome; to those he guessed would be more trouble than they could pay, he claimed to have a full building. This year of the Roman Census had brought him many more visitors than he could handle. He could afford to be choosy this season, as the travelers on the road usually filled his inn by mid-afternoon. However, he had a good heart and an open hand for people he thought were in need.

THE INNKEEPER'S WIFE

She helped Mary in her labor, later gathered the local mothers of under-two-year male babies, but was overheard by Simon Iscariot to have sighed her thanks that the mother, husband and child had gone up to Jerusalem (to present Jesus in the Temple for his circumcision), thus avoiding the death meted out to the Innocents.

SHEPHERDS

These lowly keepers of sheep in the hills above Bethlehem were witnesses to the great and joyous music coming from the heavens upon the birth of the Child, and later adored the Child with His mother in the manger of the Inn.

MAGI

These were invited by Gabriel to travel many days into the West to see the New King and to witness a great gathering of the planets above the small place called Bethlehem, built centuries before by another king named David.

AUGUSTUS CAESAR

The most powerful ruler in the known world was dream-prompted by the Angel to count all men and their possessions in his domain, raising small tax monies by selling the dyed clamshell markers in the census-count. He used the Greek way of census-taking, the distribution of leather-thonged shells to be exchanged for a silver piece upon registry with the local tax collector. The thousands of silver pieces would be returned to Rome, of course.

SIMON ISCARIOT

A forger of armor and weapons, taught in his youth by his father, Simon was very adroit in their use and therefore trained others for combat. Thus he had come to the King's attention and so became a member of Herod's court, making weapons and teaching others how to use them. He was a favorite in the court as well, having a stocky frame, fair looks, and a friendly manner. Herod occasionally sought his advice on matters of force and strategy.

LEAH

A slave girl headed for the auction block in Jerusalem, she had been bought several years before by Simon from a Samarian trader, who had mistreated her. She hated the slaver and so was grateful to her new master, Being attractive, she was frequently part of Herod's court, from which she brought news and court gossip to her master.

HEROD (AND HIGH PRIESTS)

An aging ruler, Herod's appearance was of an old, very lame man whose temperament often verged on the edge of violence toward others, even to members of his own family; he had brought about the deaths of two of his sons, for their popularity. Moreover, he had a recurring skin rash that itched constantly, adding to his usually foul mood. His advisors were frightened of him, as were the high priests of the Temple when they were summoned. They did not come eagerly into Herod's court! Although Herod was not Jewish, he ruled the Jewish people, at the pleasure of the Roman Procurator Cyrinius, of Syria. Herod's charge was to ensure that the local peace was kept by the people. His guards (several dozen allowed him by the Romans) kept the peace in the city, headed by Simon Iscariot. Most behaved well, but a few were given to local breaches of conduct by their quarreling, drinking and other misconduct.

HOLY INNOCENTS

These and their mothers were occupants of the very small, crossroads village of Bethlehem, having been recently born and circumcised in the Jewish tradition on the eighth day of their lives, as the law of Abraham required. The Innkeeper's wife knew the mothers in this small crossroads, having been midwife at each birthing. Theirs was a small community, held together by their synagogue, serving the needs of the constantly passing parade of merchants, traders, and other travelers.

THE STORY...

THE ANNUNCIATION

> In the sixth month the angel Gabriel was sent from God, to a town of Galilee named Nazareth, to a virgin betrothed to a man named Joseph, of the house of David. The virgin's name was Mary. (Luke 1:26–27)

> Now this is how the birth of Jesus Christ came about. When his Mother Mary was engaged to Joseph, but before they lived together, she was found to be with child through the power of the Holy Spirit. Joseph her husband, an upright man unwilling to expose her to the law, decided to divorce her quietly. Such was his intention when an angel of the Lord suddenly appeared in a dream and said to him, "Joseph, son of David, have no fear about taking Mary as your wife. She is to have a son and you are to name him Jesus because he will save his people from their sins. (Matthew 1:18–21)

I am called Gabriel, sent by The Most High to set the tides by which His Only Son would safely and quietly come into the world. To do this, I visited the many persons important enough to make this great event come about. Only a few of these persons have been recorded, but I sought out many others indeed, to do the bidding of The Most High! First, I knelt before a young Jewish virgin chosen long, long before by The Most High…, to whose proposal she consented, and all Heaven thrilled! In accordance with my message and to avoid scandalous gossip in synagogue, she did not think of her recent betrothal but almost immediately set off to the other side of Nazareth to visit her cousin Elizabeth, wife of the high priest Zachariah. He had been made mute ever since his heretofore barren wife had conceived and was, even now, in no less than her sixth month of expectation! There Mary "full of grace" would stay until her cousin's delivery of a son to be named John, and, at that naming, its father, Zachariah, was then freed from being tongue-tied, to the amazement of the others of his family.

EMPEROR OF THE KNOWN WORLD

In those days Caesar Augustus published a decree ordering a census of the whole world. This first census took place while Cyrinius was governor of Syria. (Luke II: 1-2)

I, Augustus Caesar, Emperor of Rome and all kingdoms and lands beyond, dreamed one night that I walked the beach near the place of my birth where Tiber flowed into the sea. In this dream I picked up many sea shells of royal purple, the color that only emperors might use! There were holes punched in the bellies of the shells and leather thongs knotted through. These were collected by the many thousands in great chests and carried up to my court. A scribe then marked down my name and the names of my wife, children and slaves, even my horse. Thus I and mine were writ down! I awoke from this dream and pondered its meaning, but not finding one I called for my advisors for interpretation. Worthless that they often are, they had none. The tidings of my dream were proclaimed beyond my court, and finally a tall, heavily cloaked man appeared to me early one evening, outlined in the setting sun. He suggested that the meaning of my dream could be interpreted, that a truly great Roman Emperor might determine how many persons could be counted in his empire, to measure the greatness of his reign. This dream then was a command for me to count all subjects of the empire, even to the lowly slaves and other properties. The sea shells had been of royal color to signify their use for an emperor only, the shells had been pierced and threaded with leather strips to hang from the necks of those who paid to be counted in all the lands of my empire. Thus all men and their families and their possessions would be recorded by my tax collectors, and thus would every free man pay his silver piece to be recorded in the place of his birth! Word of this counting-to-be would be proclaimed throughout the Empire, even to Judea and Syria and beyond. All of this to be done in the passage of one year! I, Augustus, liked the thought of silver coins in the thousands returning to my treasury, so my slaves were sent to the seashores to gather, dye purple, and thong with leather the shells to be carried in crates to the far reaches of my lands. My census year was proclaimed. Heavy would be the penalty for those failing to be counted!

IN THE KING'S SERVICE

He was talking about Judas, son of Simon the Iscariot
(John 13: 71)

I am named Simon Iscariot because I was raised in a small place called Iscarioth, in Judea. I am a Jew and follow the Law, as it has been to my benefit, even to gaining a good post in the court of King Herod of Jerusalem. By trade, I am skilled in metals, an armor-maker for His Majesty as were my father and his father before him. My knowledge is such that I train His Majesty's guards in the art of the spear, the bow and the small sword, being very adept. In these things I have prospered, even to being part of the court of King Herod.

In his court, however, I keep my tongue and counsel until asked, for it is not wise to be too sought after lest the king himself see me as a schemer and a possible enemy against him in these his older years. His sons did not live out their years as God intended, for their father summoned them to the block for treachery, treachery so well hidden that none in the court might imagine but could only fear further suspicion from their king.

This king's ill temper in his older years is caused by a great itching of his skin that none of his physicians can cure, even at peril of their lives. The itching comes and goes, especially in his nether parts, making him squirm on his great seat. His physicians lately have tried poultices of oat paste, which cools for hours at a time, dries, then must be washed away before the torment starts anew, and well before his royal temperament flares again.

Such is my view of the court of King Herod. Here I am well worked, and well rewarded for my skill. My quarters are much less than royal but comfortable enough, inhabited by my woman, Leah, and another servant. Of Leah I shall speak again.

A NEW MASTER

My master-to-be found me in the roadway where I had stumbled, my slave owner cursing me for having fallen. I returned my curses at the slaver and threw dust in his face, and the crowds howled, for though they liked what would be shown unclothed on the auction block, they cared little indeed for slavers. Then I saw him looking at us curiously, then at me only. I returned his gaze, but softly. He approached us, hand on sword hilt, asking how much the price for me at auction. They argued at length, voices rising, his sword being briefly half-drawn, then the bag of coin handed over, and my neck thong loosened, to follow him into the courtyard beyond the high gates. So I came to my new master, still unused to the ways of men, such was my worth to have been at auction! He named me Leah. I did not know him then, my new master, but I guessed at his importance in the Court. His bag of coin had been too easily handed over for me; there was more to be had!

A GOOD MAN IS
SOUGHT AFTER

> Now this is how the birth of Jesus came about. When
> his mother Mary was betrothed to Joseph, but before
> they lived together, she was found with child through
> the power of the Holy Spirit. Joseph her husband,
> an upright man unwilling to expose her to the law,
> decided to divorce her quietly. Such was his intention
> when suddenly an angel of the Lord appeared in a
> dream and said to him, "Joseph, son of David, have no
> fear about taking Mary as your wife. It is by the Holy
> Spirit that she has conceived this child. (Matthew
> 1:18 – 20)

I am named Joseph, in the lineage and heritage of the House
of David, a carpenter by calling, summoned to work my skills
in the outlying villages of the wealthy and powerful around
Nazareth. My first wife had died giving me yet another child,
and I was lonely in my grief. After some months I realized that
I could not care for my children alone. I would marry again;
thus I went to my synagogue in Nazareth to find the mar-
riage broker, for he would know which young Jewish maiden's
parents would not ask too much in gifts for their daughter.

My wish was made known to the parents of a young maid
of almost fourteen years; they were poor in property but

rich in faith and family devotion. So we were promised to each other in synagogue just before I was called away from Nazareth to the next town to work the trade for which I was well known and much respected.

When I returned some weeks later, to be wed as we had planned, her parents informed me with eyes downcast in their frightened faces that somehow my betrothed, Mary, had become with child but would not tell them the circumstance, and even now had run off to their elderly cousin Elizabeth to help her in the final months before delivering. This a birthing thought to be quite impossible in view of the older woman's many years of barrenness!

I was angry, for this breaking of betrothal was punishable by stoning for adultery according to the law of Moses. I would throw the first stone, and many more! I could see my hand in mid-air, the blood on her face! But after a time I could not keep such anger in me. I did not want her blood on my hands, so I would divorce her quietly. I hoped she would survive the gossip of her neighbors in synagogue. Divorced quietly or not, Mary would be liable to their gossip and accusations of adultery. Even then the stones might fly at her, such was the Law!

It was in those sleepy moments before dawn on a later morning that a hooded figure stood before me to whisper that my intended would give birth to the Son of the Most High! More than that, I had been chosen to care for this new child and his mother!

I pondered this half-dream, resolving to question my intended when she returned from her cousin's house on the other side of the city. A long wait it would be, before she returned to tell me of the wondrous words of that same Angel.

TO WITNESS THE KING OF ALL KINGS

It would seem a heavenly irony that the Son of the Most High is to be quietly born in an obscure, lowly place, the stable of an inn outside the great city of Jerusalem, yet there are to be fortune tellers and shepherds in worshipful attendance, under a great light shining overhead in a moonless sky. The child's mother was without sin, as had been ordained by her Creator, the Most High, perhaps even before the very beginning of all mankind. (Author)

I, Gabriel, sought out each of the star-gazers: first Melchior, then Gaspar, lastly Balthasar of Persia, finding them separately, always seeking more wealthy but gullible patrons to amaze with predictions of health and wealth in exchange for the ever appropriate coins!

To each I came in the eventide as their attendants set out maps of the stars and planets in the heavens to be seen and marked with wooden pegs in the reflecting water poured out on their star-gazing tables. To each man, in these darkened western skies I revealed the closing light of the seven unblinking stars, that would become a great light to announce the birth of the Prince of Heaven!

These heavenly lights the three were most familiar with but had not noticed their strange clustering! Each was soon eager to hasten on his way into the western horizon, to worship a great new king! After many months of travel to the west, they met by coincidence (my doing, of course), at the last caravanserai (fortress shelter for caravan travelers) the day before coming to the great gate in the eastern wall of Jerusalem. They had agreed to ask the ruler of this great city for the way to the birthplace of the new King.

STRANGERS IN THE ROAD

Everyone went to register, each to his own birthplace. And so Joseph went from the town of Nazareth in Galilee to Judea, to David's town of Bethlehem – because he was of the house and lineage of David – to register with his espoused wife, who was with child. (Luke II: 3-5)

I, Micah the Innkeeper, first saw them with the two donkeys, the first lightly burdened by the young woman, the second with woodworking tools, coming from the lowlands of the north, up the road to my inn at the last light of the winter day. Both were weary, she the worse for wear because I could see that she was already in the first pangs of her labor! Since I had no rooms left, it would have been easy to send them on. But to nowhere, for mine was the only inn! She looked at me for a long moment, silent pain in her steady eyes. I dared not wave them away!

I led them down the path around to the rear of my inn, where the other animals were feeding, under the hollowed out sandstone and coffer-beamed roof. The stranger helped me throw down clumps of hay, which he arranged for her under a cloak. This part of the stable had already been mucked out by one of my sons, so the usual animal odor was faint indeed.

They would be safe and well sheltered here, unobserved by any others.

The stranger was tall and strong looking, his arms well knotted from heavy work with the wood-working tools in the leather bags on the second donkey. His speech was gentle, his gaze straight forward in a natural dignity. He asked if he could work out the lodging coins; I showed him the pool of water around my always-leaking animal trough. And that I would move him and his wife the next day or two up the rear stone steps into a room above, after the other guests had departed for places unknown to me. There they would stay until she would present her new son at Temple in the great city just a short climb of a few miles from here, eight days from this. Strange that he was so sure of her bringing forth a son! How could he know that?

I explained that my inn was full, crowded with travelers on their way to register for the Roman census at the places of their birth, which he said that he had done on arrival with the tax collector in this small crossroads called Bethlehem. He thought his wife would deliver this night, God willing, and asked for the help of a midwife. To him I promised my own Serai, for she had helped deliver all of the children of this poor crossroads, over the years, with good success at keeping our new mothers and their babes alive. My wife was a worthy woman, with much good sense, kindness, and diligence. Though she saw (and remembered) much, few were her words to those she did not know.

I walked up the sandstone steps cut into the curved wall at the rear of the stable, up into the warm "great room" where we fed our guests, to tell my Serai of her looming midwifery! This night again would be without a moon, cool and dark under the usual clouds of this winter season. I shivered; only the shepherds would be outside, standing out in the high fields over their flocks against the slinking animal packs!

SWADDLING CLOTHS

> While they were there the days of her confinement
> were completed. She gave birth to her first-born son
> and wrapped him in swaddling cloths and laid him in
> a manger, because there was no room for them in the
> place where travelers lodged. (Luke II: 6 – 7)

Serai I am named, good wife to the innkeeper Micah. He came to the back steps of the great warming room, puffing his breath, to tell me of the new child to come, and of its parents in the shelter below. Had the day been younger, I would have sent our more drunken travelers down the steps to their rest, so that the carpenter and his wife could have a room, but there was no changing now. I went down into the shelter and pushed through the animals the carpenter had tethered around her to keep her warm.

She was a small woman of much youth. A long labor was ahead for her, I thought, and I feared she would be lost at the end! My sons brought down the jars of warmed water and the cloths woven soft for birthing.

He was a carpenter by trade, my husband had told me. Would that he had been a shepherd, knowing about the birth of sheep at the least! He would not be of much help; I asked him to hold his wife's hands and to wipe her brow. This he did, gently and steadily, whispering to her. In between her pains in silence she looked out to the growing brightness, yet I knew this was not the time of the moon.

Bright light reflected inward from the water pooled around the leaking trough. So very strange this night was becoming! How odd she did not cry out; did she fear that she would wake the other travelers in their rooms above?

Hours later, not too long after midnight, her son was born, and I made him comfortable in the warm cloths. The girl, for that was what she was, seemed very peaceful, great happiness in her face. She held her child close to her heart, cooing to him again and again and more! The carpenter was beaming as he went outside into the light, to look up into the bright sky. It was then I heard the wondrous music and all manner of voices, in high and low tones they were singing. How could this be? What did this mean?

Later, the carpenter came back, three shepherds following him inside to kneel before the child and his mother. They spoke fearfully of a great opening in the sky above, of marvelous singing, in the light shining down from the moonless sky, and of the bright figure that suddenly appeared before them out in their hills to tell them of the birth of a great king! Their voices were hushed, almost frightened, describing the great music they had heard from the sky above.

Now there was no other sound except for the breathing of the animals. I went up the steps to the warming room where my husband was snoring on a bench. I woke him to tell of these strange doings below and outside. He grunted and cautioned me to leave these things alone. I pulled him up and pushed him off to our own pallets.

THE VISITORS

> After Jesus' birth in Bethlehem of Judea during the
> reign of King Herod, astrologers from the east arrived
> one day inquiring, "Where is the newborn king of the
> Jews? We observed his star at its rising and have come
> to pay him homage." (Matthew II: 1-2)

My master is quite puzzled; he was summoned from his work
early this morning by Herod's chief advisor. The three strangers and their well-armed attendants appeared late in the
morning at the eastern gate for admittance to the Court, to
see anyone who could tell them where the King of all Kings
would be born.

My master said that the three might be from Cathay in the
east! Or places not quite so far. They were richly dressed, their
attendants and camels likewise adorned. Their words about a
"King of all Kings" were alarming to my master, for he feared
that his lord, King Herod, might be less than pleased. Much
less! My master might have to escort them from the city, but
to where? No one seems to know of this "King of all Kings."

WORDS OF A LONG-AGO PROPHET

> At this news King Herod became greatly disturbed, and with him all Jerusalem. Summoning all the chief priests and scribes of the people, he inquired of them where the Messiah was to be born. Herod called the Astrologers aside and found out from them the exact time of the star's appearance. Then he sent them down to Bethlehem, after having instructed them: "Go and get detailed information about the child. When you have found him, report it to me so that I may go and offer him homage, too." (Matthew II: 3-4; 7-8)

After much discussion among the court nobles, the decision was made to grant the visitors entrance into the court. The King himself would be awakened from his mid-day sleep and so informed of the strangers and their questioning words. He came into the court area, heard once again the strangers' requests, then called for the high priest and his attending priests.

The message was repeated! There were more questions and more vague answers, while an increasingly angry Herod began shouting at the priests to open their scrolls and find any words about "king of kings." Or their heads…! They quickly ran out from the royal rage, heads down and eyes shielded.

. FREDERICK CLINTON BURDICK .

Finally, hours later, the priests returned to the court, and Herod was called again; the three travelers were summoned from their tents outside the walls. Others, including myself, were once more summoned in haste. Clearly the priests were very frightened, their hands shook, holding the scrolls; Herod screamed his command at them to speak. They began their story, as follows: A prophet of more than seven centuries earlier had made an obscure reference to a small crossroads town called Bethlehem, of the making by another king, named David, lying less than half a day's walk toward the western sea at the crossroads to the north and south. Certainly there was no king to be found there, Herod announced to the entire court.

The three visitors stepped away to talk in whispers, while I watched carefully. They approached the throne once more to say that they had traveled long from their very far lands; they would go back to their tents, and in the morning they would go down the short distance to the crossroads to see what could be found.

Herod was silent for many minutes; he would look first at the three visitors, then to his priests, and back again to the three strangers. Now a searching look at me, his armor-maker. Then, chin in hand, a long dark gaze at the stone floor, then to the visitors and once again to me! Now, in so sweetened a voice that I, Simon Iscariot, could not recognize, Herod spoke. When the three men returned to tell him of their success in finding the child, he himself would go and worship this new king. He grimaced, then laughed nervously. Again a sidelong glance at me that shook me greatly!

. 46 .

He arose from the throne seat, this time without the help of his attendant, and descended the steps to embrace each visitor. He left the throne room on the arm of his attendant, shuffling along but resisting the urge to scratch himself. The entourage of visitors and their attendants quickly hurried out of the castle to their tents. It was clear that they had not been impressed favorably. They looked neither right nor left and said little, to avoid being overheard. I guessed that their tents would be even more carefully guarded this night.

CHAPTER XI LEAH

PRESENT FEARS
AND PAST ONES

> God had also said to Abraham: On your part, you and
> your descendants after you must keep my covenant
> throughout the ages. This is my covenant with you and
> your descendants after you that you must keep: every
> male among you shall be circumcised. Circumcise the
> flesh of the foreskin, and that shall be the mark of the
> covenant between you and me. (Genesis XVII: 9 – 11)

My master returned, throwing himself down on the mat that
served him at night. I sensed that he was very troubled by the
day's happenings, particularly by the long glances that Herod
had sent his way. I raised myself from my mat to his and moved
gently to his side. I saw his eyes open to look me, then slowly
close once more in deep study. I also had thoughts, but of an
earlier time.

I was glad that the slave master had kept me a maiden,
to fetch a better price on the auction block. His sheathed
uncleanliness could have wrought sickness in me, from
which I, like so many other women in the same circumstance, might perish. But to him, my new owner, I had
given myself freely, not one tear shed. He was kind and
gentle, always. We talked in whispers about the visitors and

FREDERICK CLINTON BURDICK

our king; did Herod really mean to visit the new "King of Kings"? I was suddenly afraid; he had looked too often and long at my master. Too long not to have been scheming!

AMIDST THE MUSIC AND LIGHT

There were shepherds in that locality, living in the fields and keeping night watch by turns over their flocks. The angel of the Lord appeared to them as the glory of the Lord shone around them, and they were very much afraid. The angel said to them: You have nothing to fear! I come to proclaim good news to you —tidings of great joy to be shared by the whole people. This day in David's city a savior has been born to you: in a manger you will find an infant wrapped in swaddling clothes. Suddenly there was with the angel a multitude of the heavenly host, praising God and saying, "Glory to God in high heaven, peace on earth to those on whom his favor rests." (Luke 2: 8-14)

We saw the angel, standing just beyond the rock wall of the sheepfold, the animals lying quietly together in the light that streamed down through the break in the winter clouds from the great star overhead. The angel spoke of a new king born that very night at the road-crossing below, in the manger of the inn. He would have us hurry down through the meadows to see for ourselves, while he would watch over the animals. Such was his shining face, such was his exultant voice that we dared not tarry!

As we climbed down over and around the rocks, the sky split open, it seemed, and there was music both high and low, and great voices sang out in praise of The Most High. Sights and sounds to remember all our days! Then we were in the manger cave, bowing low before the child and his mother. Such happiness on her face, such peacefulness! We presented the new lamb born (so strangely out of season!) earlier that day.

STRANGE ARE THE VISITORS

After their audience with the king, they set out. The star which they had observed at its rising went ahead of them until it came to a standstill over the place where the child was. They were overjoyed at seeing the star, and on entering the house, found the child with Mary his mother. They prostrated themselves and did him homage. Then they opened their coffers and presented him with gifts of gold, frankincense, and myrrh.

(Matthew 2: 9-11)

The day after the child was born, I saw the carpenter outside the stable looking at that old water trough, pacing up the hill to the small stream that came down and then abruptly turned away to splash into the deep gorge on the other side. The wood of my trough has rotted. Can he repair it? This carpenter clearly has something different in mind.

My sons must fill the old trough both morning and night to water the camels and donkeys tethered nearby during the day and under the thatch at night. Will he stay long enough? Clearly, his wife cannot be moved yet into a room that lies at the rear of my inn. She is still weak from her birthing, which my Serai said was done in the quiet, broken only by her almost silent whimpers. Very, very strange, these doings! But my wife is very much taken with this new mother. As I have already said, she has much good sense.

Then, in the midst of my thoughts, a commotion in the roadway! The usual pilgrims had been pushed aside by the guards of a long entourage. Three men came riding on their adorned camels, surrounded by their personal guards in matching livery, all in silence, mind you. I saw the richness of their dress, the silver mountings on the animals' harness. The attendants threw coins beyond the crowd that gathered and then ran out of the way after the silver. To my wonder, the camels entered the compound of my inn (I had thought they would take the northern or southern road). Down they sprang and tethered the animals to stakes hammered into the dirt. Quickly three tents were set up against the afternoon chill and just as quickly were occupied by the three visitors. Their attendants squatted in the dust outside, clearly as ready to defend as to serve.

My wife Serai came down the stone steps into the stable from the great room above and helped the young mother prepare herself and her newborn son. Was she expecting these strangers? Her husband, the carpenter, seemed speechless, but he stood in front of the stable opening as though he would defend his wife and the child. I saw no cause for alarm; the afternoon silence was deep.

After a time, the tents suddenly opened and the three kings, for that is what we came to call them, approached the stable and peered in. The three bowed low, then to my amazed eyes they knelt in the dirt! Their words were softly spoken, as small bags were brought out of the wide sleeves of their garments and placed before the mother and child. These were quickly gathered up by the carpenter and carried out of sight. The young mother appeared to understand her visitors, for she nodded her head and even laughed with them. How was it that she could understand them? The carpenter silently looked on. My wife stood by, completely speechless for once!

THE DEPARTURE

Yesterday the Magi, for that is what I called them, came down from the city and pitched their tents on our dirt near the stable. They greeted the carpenter and his young wife, and then gifted them too! Today they were up before the sun, their tents packed away on the camels by the guards. The column rode slowly out to the crossroads, where I could see a hooded man blocking their way. He spoke softly to the three, pointing up to the city walls and shaking his head, then nodding to the north road and then to the south. Suddenly two of the Magi began the road to the north, as if to far Antioch, while the third Magus went up to the crown of the road and then down, now out of sight, toward Egypt.

Tonight, having an empty room, my husband moved the carpenter and his wife and the child up the steps to a rear room beyond the great warming space. Outside, the water trough was new, and a hollowed tree branch brought water from the stream down into the trough for the animals. My sons are happy that they have been released from their water jar chores of the morning and late afternoon. Such clever work by the carpenter for only the price of a room!

THE SEARCH

My master was summoned early this morning to go before the King. When he returned, he told me that King Herod had given him the task of finding the three strangers near Bethlehem and returning them to the court, to be questioned. The king was very angry in his words. His patience of these three days has left him! My master is to take a dozen spear men to escort the three wise men back through the western gate. He armed himself without a word, his mood was so dark. I am frightened. What if he should not return?

THE VISITORS GONE!

His Highness, my king, has ordered the return of the three travelers to the court. He would feast them well, and all their entourage, as he badly wanted the details about the birth of a "new king of kings."

I rode horseback to the crossroads some half-dozen miles down from the southern gate, not a long time in the saddle. I went directly to the inn because the innkeeper and his wife always eyed the travelers on the north and south roads. They wanted to fill their rooms. From them I learned little, except that the three strangers and their guards had left right at sunrise two days earlier, to take the north and south roads, not back up the hill to the nearest gate of the city! The innkeeper could tell me nothing more. His inn looked empty and silent. I did not like the report that I would have to make on my return to my king. I feared his anger might spill over on the messenger!

THE PLANNING

My master returned late that afternoon to the court, to make his report to King Herod. He came to me later and said he would return to Bethlehem the next day, to seek out those boys born in the last two years! He told me only this, but I could see he had more to say. I did not ask. His darkened face told me that he would not answer!

Again this night he drank with the King before coming to his bed. He smelled. I pretended to be asleep. By midmorning he was up and clothed in the King's colors, and well armed, too! I did not ask why, before he left. I have a great fear in me.

CHAPTER XVIII SIMON

THE PLOT

> Once Herod realized that he had been deceived by the
> astrologers, he became furious. He ordered the mas-
> sacre of all the boys two years and under in Bethlehem
> and its environs, making his calculations on the basis
> of the date he had learned from the astrologers.
> (Matthew 2: 16)

This day I turned my horse once more toward the crossroads,
to see the innkeeper. He and his wife were busy seeing off
the night's guests, tending to their animals and collecting the
coins for their stay at the inn.

Finally, I talked to the wife, Serai her name. Her eyes were
very quick, but kept downward to the ground. Surely my
royal uniform would not threaten her this much, but she was
hard to talk to. I asked her again and again about the three
strangers but gained nothing. They had come there, raised
their tents, stayed the night and brought them down the next
morning, then left just as promptly. Nothing more! Was she
stupid or cunning not to know more?

Then I asked her whether there were many children in
this small crossroads town. There were not many, but she had
helped bring them out of their mothers into the world, as the
good midwife to all who needed her. How many under the
age of two, I wanted to know. About a dozen girls and boys,

she thought. I asked further if the boys had been properly cared for under the law, circumcised if Jewish, and she said yes. Yes, the rabbi of their synagogue in this small crossroads had done the cutting, the boys small but properly noisy on the eighth day of their lives, before their beaming parents.

And so I laid my king's plan upon her. King Herod, I said, was most interested in their circumcisions, that they had been done properly, of course! I asked if she would be able to gather the boys under two years, and their mothers, at her inn, to be rewarded if such circumcisions had been done well under the law. Yes, she would have them at her inn in a day's time! I said that I would return on that morning with friends who would inspect and judge, and give rewards for the cuttings.

A GREAT CRY TO COME

> What was said through Jeremiah the prophet was then fulfilled: "A cry was heard at Ramah, sobbing and loud lamentation: Rachel bewailing her children; no comfort for her, since they are no more." (Matthew 2: 17 – 18)

My wife was both excited and upset. for she was trying hard to remember which boys she had delivered in the past two years to be circumcised at synagogue. Although she did not speak to the rabbi, she finally had a small list of just six boys under two years, whose mothers she would invite the next day at noon, to show off their sons' circumcisions. To this soldier of King Herod! For rewards, too! They would gather in the great room above the stable. My wife was bursting with pride over the fruits of her midwifery.

THE SEVENTH CHILD

Tomorrow a great day in little Bethlehem! There are only six boys under two years born with my help, and alive still. It is too bad that my newest little one just born, the seventh lad, can not be here. Tomorrow his parents will take him up the road to the southern gate and into the city, to be presented at the great temple. There the law of Abraham will be fulfilled as required on his eighth day of life. Poor lad, he will miss the business here. I shall not tell his parents, lest they have disappointment.

IN THE DETAILS, THE EVIL

The king has spoken—my orders are to take with me my two most troublesome palace guards. I know them well! Slovenly, lazy, frequently too sick from last night's drunkenness. No court uniforms for them, only for me. Clean tunics without palace insignia; no swords shall they carry, but short knives to do their work. And I with my sword to do mine! They will follow behind my horse to the crossroads inn this morning to enter the stable, then up the steps to the great room. There I shall pour them wine until noon when the boys under two shall be brought in by their beaming, excited mothers.

They will know what to do, on my command, then down the rear steps to the turning along the wall, where my blade will be waiting. My king does not want these two to return to the palace with unusual tales! But their bodies? I have no plans for those, yet.

THE INNOCENTS AWAITED

I saw them before they reached the crossroads, the two on foot in plain tunics, following the man on horseback, he dressed in court colors. They came into the great room from the rear steps leading up from the manger. Their leader talked briefly, then returned to the top step and waited. They drank their wine at the long table, not speaking, grimness in their faces, waiting. My wife stood at the front steps of the inn, a great smile on her face to welcome the six mothers and their tiny sons.

HOW COULD THIS HAPPEN!

My lady and her new son and husband left the gate at first light, she on the one animal and he leading that and the other burdened with their goods and his tools. I waited almost to the noon sun, as planned. My neighbor wives in the village brought their newest sons into the inn with much anticipation. The boys' perfect circumcisions would be much admired, I was sure! They lined up before the two men, who slowly got to their feet.

Then a shouted command came up from the rear stairs, knives flashed, the bleeding, the women's gasps of horror, and then their screams! The two men ran to the stairs, colliding, running downward. Then grunting, and then wheezing sounds below. I ran out to find my husband, then chased after the women holding their dying infants in blood-soaked arms. Out of the inn they went, never to return, never to speak or even to look into my face again! I followed after, trying to assure them that this was a horrible mistake that my husband and I had known nothing about. Their shrieks of grief muffled their replies; my ears were the better for that.

I followed my Micah back to the great room. As he started down the rear steps, I called to him my thought how fortunate that my lady and her son had escaped all this horror because he was off to be circumcised. As my husband went further down the steps, we heard the horse galloping off, up to the crossroads and onward up to the city looming not far above us.

There were two men lying in the blood from their slashed throats on the floor of the stable, silenced forever. They had to be gotten rid of, or our inn was finished, and we with it! Micah and our two sons pulled both monsters out into the yard, then on past the new water trough, upward to the stream and over into the ravine below. The night animals would be busy well before the next dawn.

SIMEON AND ANA: BLESSINGS FOREVER!

There lived in Jerusalem at the time a certain man named Simeon. He was just and pious, and awaited the consolation of Israel, and the Holy Spirit was upon him. It was revealed to him by the Holy Spirit that he would not experience death until he had seen the Anointed of the Lord. He came to the temple now, inspired by the Spirit, and when the parents brought in the child Jesus to perform for him the customary ritual of the law, he took him in his arms and blessed God with these words: "Now, Master, you can dismiss your servant in peace; you have fulfilled your word. For my eyes have witnessed your saving deed displayed for all the peoples to see: A revealing light to the Gentiles, the glory of your people Israel." (Luke 2: 25 – 32)

I could not believe my ears, standing below the stone steps. Was there a seventh child, one who'd been at the inn all along? My former guardsmen could fend for themselves, bleeding heavily from throat wounds as they were. Their leaving so abruptly was no loss to me! I found my horse outside near the water trough and quickly headed for the crossroads for the trip back up to the city.

If I could find them, perhaps at the temple. I would be able to make another plan. I would follow them and complete my king's business before nightfall. Only then might I return to my work, to my Leah, and to safety. My thoughts were racing – why did my king order the two guards dead but no harm be done to the mothers of the six boys? What was his plan? Then another thought came like a lightning flash: how did his plan end for me?

When I reached the temple, I inquired whether there had been young boys presented to the priests today, and yes, there had been. An old man told me that he would soon die, as The Most High had promised him that he would see the Messiah before his final moment. And this day, be praised, he had witnessed the presentation and circumcision of the Lord! On and on he went, along with a old woman who wept that she too had seen the child and its mother, and her husband! Yes, the child had left with his parents; they would be returning to the northern town of Nazareth.

I left the temple, found my horse, and returned the way I had come, back through the afternoon crowds, out the western gate and down the road. It did not take long for my horse to carry me to the crossroads. I wanted to turn north for Nazareth, but the animal needed water! So once more I crossed over into the inn's courtyard and made to the rear where the water trough was located, pushing my horse in among those animals already brought in by the travelers for the night. No one was around; all was quiet. The innkeeper and his wife were inside settling their newest guests. I led my horse out to the main road and looked off in the distance. There they were! Not down the north road, but on the south road climbing to its crown before beginning the descent down into Egypt.

As I lifted my leg up to the stirrup, a crushing weight fell on my back and shoulders, the air rushing out of my chest, slamming me into my horse so hard that the animal grunted and side-stepped to avoid falling. My face was tipped to the side, my right eye could see just beyond the saddle edge where the impossibly long, shining sword pointed outward in the direction of that road. Drops of light seemed to follow along its edge, upward to its point. My eye followed, and I could just see the man leading the one animal with the woman, and the other following, heavily burdened.

They disappeared over the crown of that road. The road was empty, but the voice filled my ear, words of warning that I would never forget, terrible echoing sounds that went right through me. I hear them still:

> *"Come not near the Child and His mother*
> *lest you burn in the now than the later!"*

Then I was alone, barely hanging off the horn of my saddle. I must have slipped to the ground, senseless. Hours later, in the darkness on that road, I decided that I would follow the same road into Egypt. I dared not return to Herod's court. My livelihood there was finished, but I had my life and my trade. I would survive.

EPILOGUE

Simon Iscariot escaped Herod's search for him by going down to Egypt, where after a time of profitable metalworking, he married a widowed Jewess. She bore him a son whom he named Judas. For the remainder of his life, Simon was close to Judas, whom he brought back to Judea, to live in a small village called Iscarioth.

It was from Simon that Judas learned that the Messiah had already been born, that this messiah could mean the end of the Roman rule of the Jewish people; thus Judas should look for and perhaps follow this "promised one."

Judas is several years short of his third decade when he sets out to look for "The Messiah." His direction is northward to the Jordan. He will first seek a man named John, a prophet of The Most High. Later, he will ask to follow the man known as the Nazarene.

But that is a story for someone else to tell.

SOURCES

Raymond E Brown, S.S., *The Birth of the Messiah, A Commentary on the Infancy Narratives in the Gospels of Matthew and Luke* (New York: Doubleday1977, 1993)

Gospels of Matthew, Luke and Mark, *The New American Bible* (New York: Catholic Book Publishing Co., July, 1970)

Stephen M. Miller, *The Complete Guide to the Bible* (Uhrichsville, Ohio: Barbour Publishing Co., 2007)

Denis O'Shea, *The First Christmas* (Milwaukee: The Bruce Publishing Co., 1962)